PlayTime® Piano

Rock 'n Roll

2010 EDITION

Level 1

5-Finger Melodies

This book belongs to: _____

Arranged by

Nancy and Randall Faber

Production Coordinator: Jon Ophoff
Design and Illustration: Terpstra Design, San Francisco
Engraving: Dovetree Productions, Inc.

FABER
PIANO ADVENTURES®

3042 Creek Drive
Ann Arbor, Michigan 48108

D1275421

A NOTE TO TEACHERS

PlayTime® Piano Rock 'n Roll is a collection of rock and roll classics from the '50s and '60s. Selections such as *Blue Suede Shoes* and *Rock Around the Clock* bring back memories for parents and teachers. *The Purple People Eater, Rockin' Robin,* and *Peanut Butter* give this book a special appeal to the young piano student. The selections offer fun and excitement at the lesson, while still providing practice in the basics.

PlayTime® Piano Rock 'n Roll is part of the *PlayTime® Piano* series arranged by Faber and Faber. "PlayTime" designates Level 1 of the *PreTime® to BigTime® Piano Supplementary Library* and is available in a variety of musical styles: *Popular, Classics, Favorites, Rock 'n Roll, Jazz & Blues, Hymns, Children's Songs,* and *Christmas.*

Following are the levels of the supplementary library, which lead from *PreTime®* to *BigTime®*.

PreTime® Piano	(Primer Level)
PlayTime® Piano	(Level 1)
ShowTime® Piano	(Level 2A)
ChordTime® Piano	(Level 2B)
FunTime® Piano	(Level 3A – 3B)
BigTime® Piano	(Level 4)

Each level offers books in a variety of styles, making it possible for the teacher to offer stimulating material for every student. For a complimentary detailed listing, e-mail faber@pianoadventures.com or write us at the mailing address below.

Visit **www.PianoAdventures.com**.

Teacher Duets

Optional teacher duets are a valuable feature of the *PlayTime® Piano* series. Although the arrangements stand complete on their own, the duets provide a fullness of harmony and rhythmic vitality. And not incidentally, they offer the opportunity for parent and student to play together.

Helpful Hints:

1. The student should know his or her part thoroughly before the teacher duet is used. However, the teacher can effectively use the duet to demonstrate the meter and musical style.

2. Rehearsal numbers are provided to give the student and teacher starting places.

3. The teacher may wish to count softly a measure aloud before beginning, as this will help the ensemble.

ISBN 978-1-61677-019-8

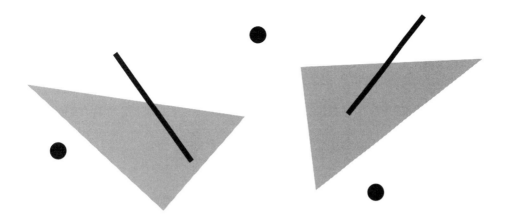

TABLE OF CONTENTS

Rock Around the Clock

Words and Music by
MAX C. FREEDMAN and JIMMY DeKNIGHT

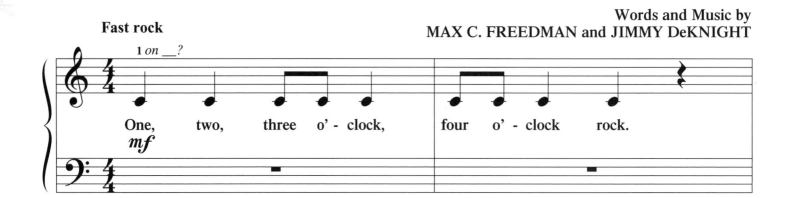

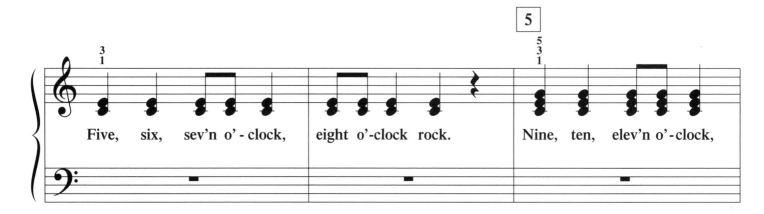

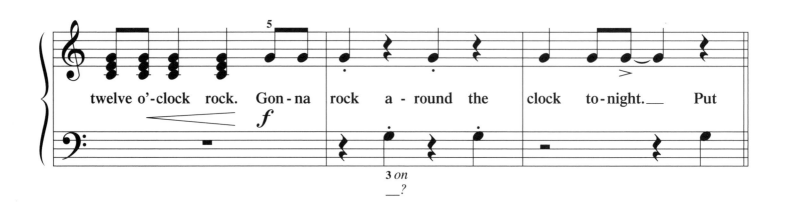

Teacher Duet: (Student plays 1 octave higher)

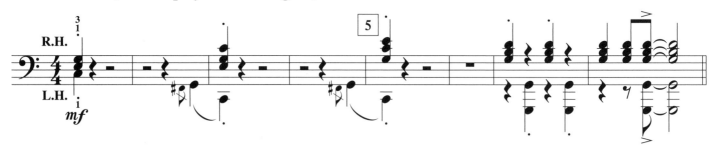

Surfer Girl

Words and Music by
BRIAN WILSON

Rather slowly

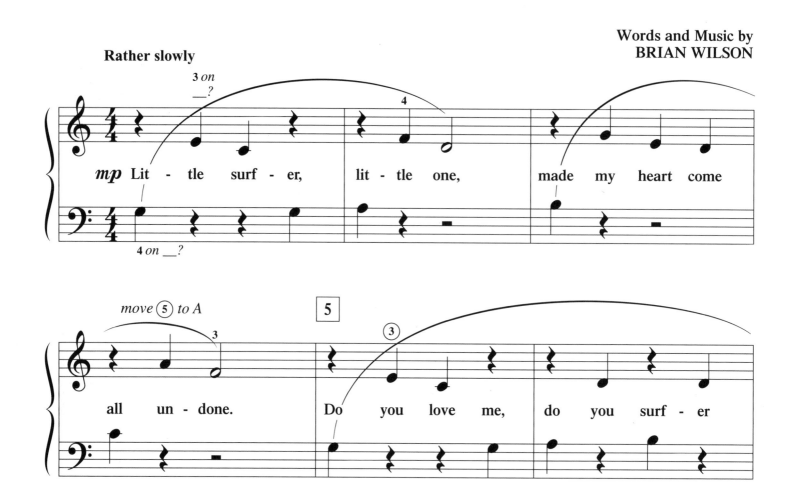

Teacher Duet: (Student plays 1 octave higher)

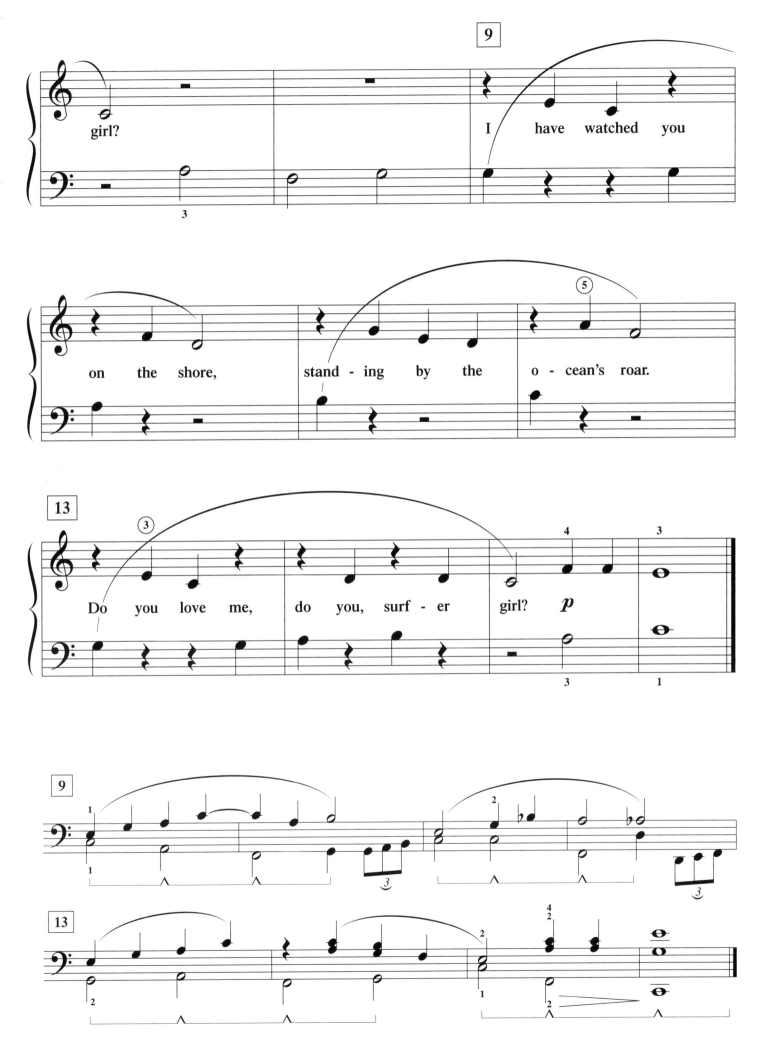

Rockin' Robin

Words and Music by
J. THOMAS and LEON RENE

Bright and fast

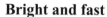

Teacher Duet: (Student plays 1 octave higher)

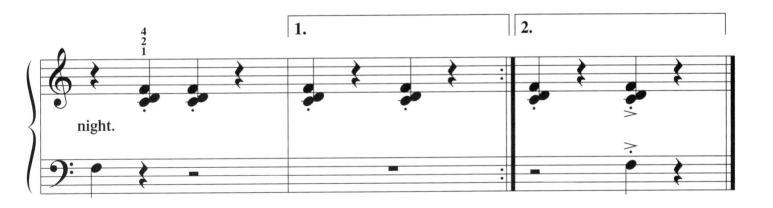

The Green Mosquito

By ARTHUR ROBERTS
and ARTHUR WANDER

Buzzing fast!

Teacher Duet: (Student plays as written)

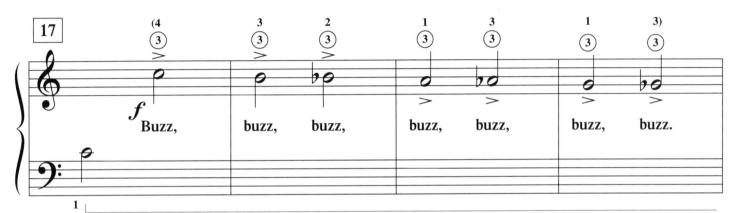

(Teacher pedals for the duet.)

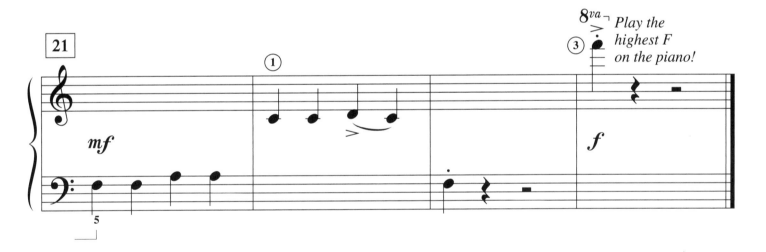

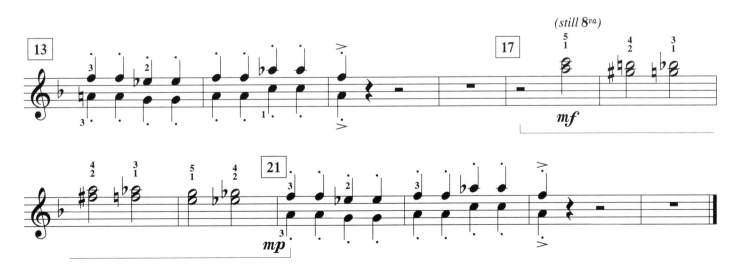

FF1019

Teacher's Note: The rhythm of measure 2 may be taught by rote.
(Tap or clap, then play.)

Cool Strut

RANDALL FABER

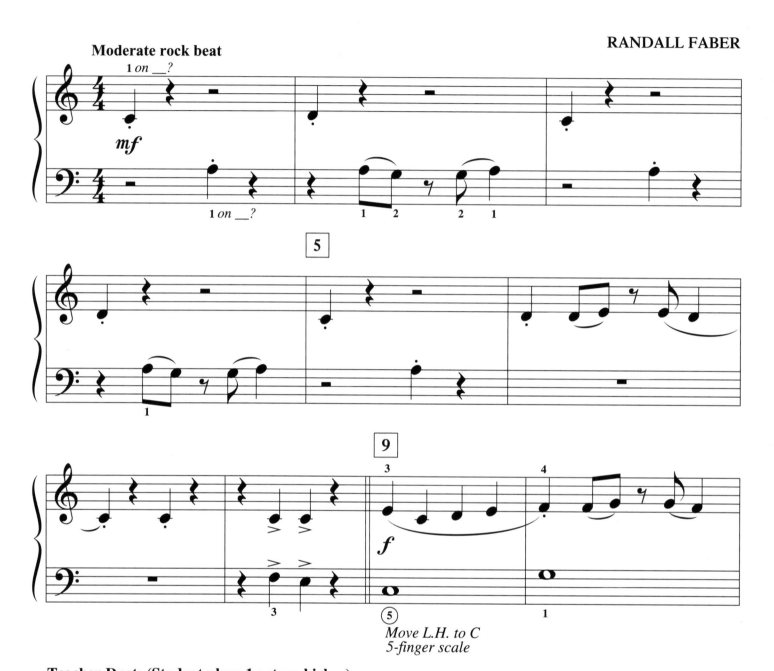

Teacher Duet: (Student plays 1 octave higher)

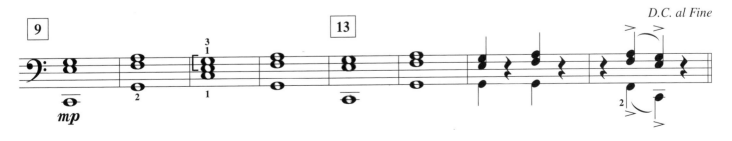

Come Go With Me

Words and Music by
C.E. QUICK

The Purple People Eater

Words and Music by
SHEB WOOLEY

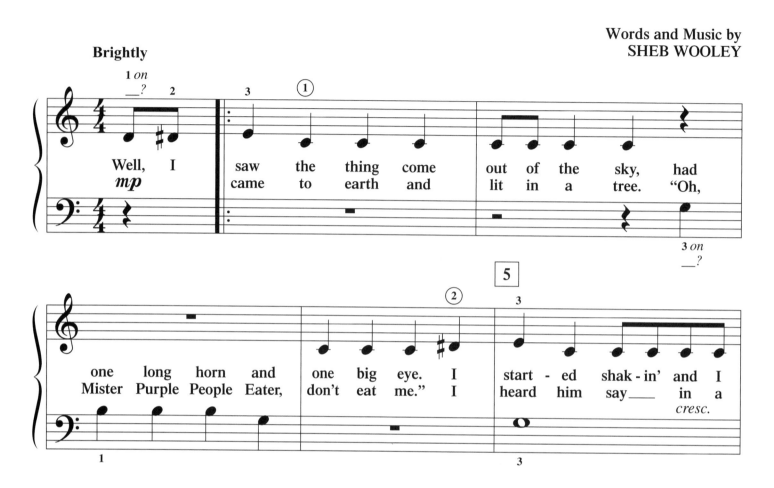

Well, I / saw the thing come / out of the sky, had
came to earth and / lit in a tree. "Oh,

one long horn and / one big eye. I / start - ed shak - in' and I
Mister Purple People Eater, / don't eat me." I / heard him say___ in a

Teacher Duet: (Student plays 1 octave higher)

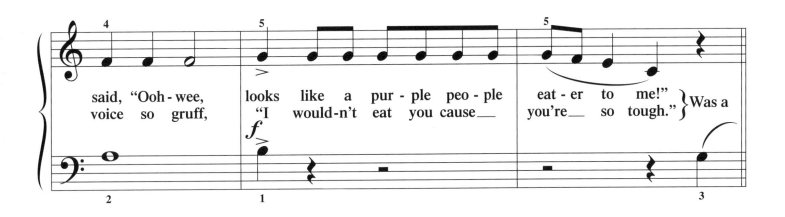

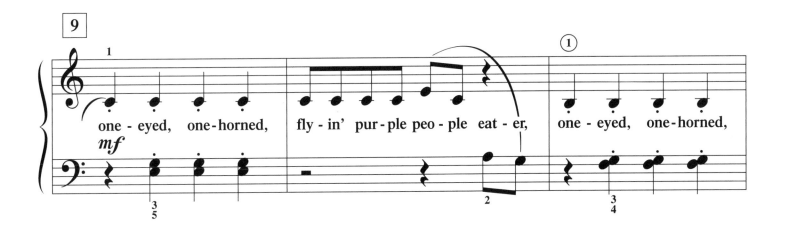

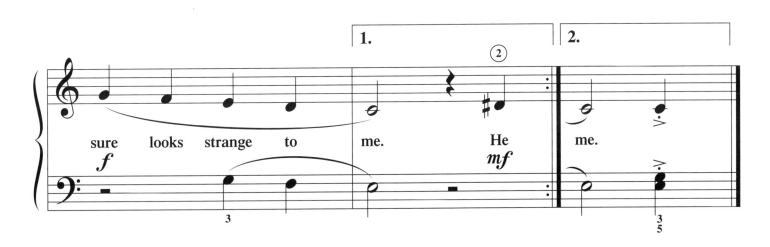

Walk Right In

Words and Music by
GUS CANNON and **H. WOODS**

Peanut Butter

Words and Music by
**SMITH, GOLDSMITH,
BARNUM, and COOPER**

Teacher Duet: (Student plays 1 octave higher)

Blue Suede Shoes

Words and Music by
CARL LEE PERKINS